LOL

EASTER JOKES

FOR KIDS

How do you catch the Easter Bunny?

Hide in the bushes and make a noise like a carrot!

Do you know how bunnies stay in shape?

Hare-obics.

What kind of jewelry do rabbits wear?

14 carrot gold.

What's the difference between a bunny and a lumberjack?

One chews and hops, the other hews and chops.

How does
the Easter Bunny
say Happy Easter?

Hoppy Easter!

Why did the magician have to cancel his show?

He'd just washed his hare and couldn't do a thing with it.

What type of movie is about water fowl?

A duckumentary.

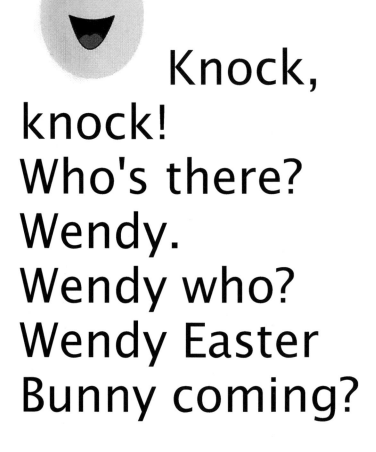 Knock, knock!
Who's there?
Wendy.
Wendy who?
Wendy Easter Bunny coming?

What is the difference between a crazy bunny and a counterfeit bill?

One is bad money and the other is a mad bunny!

What's long and stylish and full of cats?

The Easter Purr-ade!

What is the end of Easter?

The letter R.

What do you call a duck that just doesn't fit in?

Mallardjusted.

Why is the letter A like a flower?

A bee comes after it.

Why did the egg go to the baseball game?

For the egg-stra innings!

What happened when the Easter Bunny met the rabbit of his dreams?

They lived hoppily ever after!

What do you call rabbits that marched in a long sweltering Easter parade?

Hot, cross bunnies.

What is the Easter Bunny's favorite state capital?

Albunny, New York!

What do you call an egg from outer space?

An "Egg-stra terrestial".

What would you get if you crossed the Easter Bunny with a famous French general?

Napoleon Bunnyparte!

What is the Easter Bunny's favourite sport?

Basket-ball, of course!

Why didn't the Easter egg cross the road?

Because he wasn't a chicken yet!

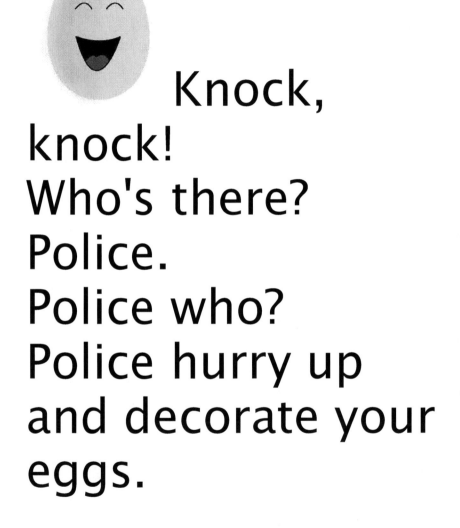 Knock, knock!
Who's there?
Police.
Police who?
Police hurry up and decorate your eggs.

Where does the Easter Bunny go when he needs a new tail?

To a re-tail store!

Who is the Easter Bunny's favorite movie actor?

Rabbit De Niro!

What kind of jokes do eggs tell?

Egg yolks!

Does the Easter Bunny like baseball?

Oh, yes. He's a rabbit fan!

What would you get if you crossed the Easter Bunny with an overstressed person?

An Easter basket case!

What's yellow, has long ears, and grows on trees?

The Easter Bunana!

Why are you stuffing all that Easter candy into your mouth?"

"Because it doesn't taste as good if I stuff it in my ears."

Did you hear the one about the Easter Bunny who sat on a bee?

It's a tender tail!

Why was the bird sitting in the Easter basket?

She was trying to hatch her peanut butter eggs!

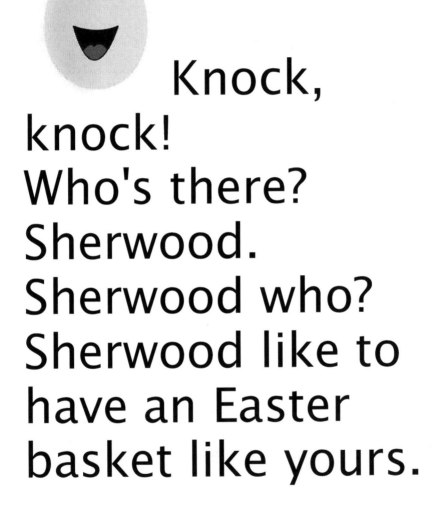 Knock, knock!
Who's there?
Sherwood.
Sherwood who?
Sherwood like to have an Easter basket like yours.

What do you need if your chocolate eggs mysteriously disappear?

You need an eggsplanation!

What's big and purple and hugs your Easter basket?

The Easter Barney!

How does the Easter Bunny paint all of those eggs?

He hires Santa's elves during the off-season.

How does the Easter Bunny stay in shape?

He does lots of hare-obics.

What sport are the eggs good at?

Running!

What's the difference between the Easter Bunny and a boy who fails at school?

One's a hare-head and the other's an air-head!

What would you get if you crossed the Easter Bunny with Chinese food?

Hop suey!

Why was the father Easter egg so strict?

He was hard-boiled.

Where does the Easter Bunny study medicine?

John Hop-kins.

What did the mommy egg say to the baby egg?

You're "Egg-stra special".

Knock, knock! Who's there? Howard. Howard who? Howard you like a chocolate bunny?

Decorate an egg and give it to someone egg-stra special!

Decorate an egg and give it to someone egg-stra special!

Decorate an egg and give it to someone egg-stra special!

Decorate an egg and give it to someone egg-stra special!

Decorate an egg and give it to someone egg-stra special!

Decorate an egg and give it to someone egg-stra special!

38556637R00035

Made in the USA
Middletown, DE
09 March 2019